The Unaccompanied

The Unaccompanied

{*Poems*}

SIMON ARMITAGE

ALFRED A. KNOPF   NEW YORK   2017

THIS IS A BORZOI BOOK
PUBLISHED BY ALFRED A. KNOPF

Published in the United States by Alfred A. Knopf,
a division of Penguin Random House LLC, New York,
and distributed in Canada by Random House of Canada,
a division of Penguin Random House Canada Limited, Toronto.
Originally published in hardcover in Great Britain by
Faber & Faber Ltd, London, in 2017.

www.aaknopf.com

Library of Congress Cataloging-in-Publication Data
Names: Armitage, Simon, 1963– author.
Title: The unaccompanied / by Simon Armitage.
Description: First Edition. | New York : Alfred A. Knopf, 2017.
Identifiers: LCCN 2017021893 (print) | LCCN 2017007454 (ebook) |
ISBN 9781524732424 (hardcover) | ISBN 9781524732431 (ebook)
Classification: LCC PR6051.R564 A6 2017 (ebook) | LCC PR6051.R564 (print) |
DDC 821/.914—dc23
LC record available at https://lccn.loc.gov/2017007454

Front-of-jacket photograph by Michael Monteaux/plainpicture
Jacket design by Carol Devine Carson

Manufactured in the United States of America
First American Edition

For Sue

Acknowledgments

Acknowledgments are due to the following newspapers, magazines, journals, and books, in which many of the poems first appeared:

Ash, Axon (Australia), *Best British Poetry 2014* (Salt, 2014), *Edinburgh Review, Fiddlehead* (Canada), *Granta, Guardian, London Review of Books, New Statesman, The New Yorker, The North, Oxford Poetry, Ploughshares, Plume, PN Review, Poetry, Poetry Ireland Review, Poetry London, Poetry Review, The Sheffield Anthology: Poems from the City Imagined* (Smith | Doorstop), *Times Literary Supplement,* and *Wenlock Poetry Festival Anthology 2011* (Ellingham Press, 2011).

Versions of four of the poems were originally published in *The Motorway Service Station as a Destination in Its Own Right* (Smith | Doorstop, 2009).

"The Present" received the 2010 Keats-Shelley Prize for Poetry.

Contents

The Unaccompanied

Last Snowman

He drifted south
    down an Arctic seaway
        on a plinth of ice, jelly tots

weeping lime-green tears
    around both eyes,
        a carrot for a nose

(some reported parsnip),
    below which a clay pipe
        drooped from a mouth

that was pure stroke victim.
    A red woolen scarf trailed
        in the meltwater drool

at his base, and he slumped
    to starboard, kinked,
        gone at the pelvis.

From the buffet deck
    of a passing cruise liner
        stag and hen parties shied

Scotch eggs and Pink Ladies
    as he rounded the stern.
        He sailed on between banks

of rubberneckers
    and camera lenses
        into a bloodshot west,

past islands vigorous
    with sunflower and bog myrtle,
        singular and abominable.

The Present

I shove up through the old plantation—larch
out of season, drab, drained of all greenness,
widowed princesses in moth-eaten furs—
and stride out onto the lap of the moor.
Rotten and rusted, a five-bar gate
lies felled in the mud, letting the fields escape.

Winter is late and light this year, thin snow
half puddled, sun still trapped in the earth,
sludge underfoot all the way to the ridge.

And no sign of the things I came here to find,
except in a high nick at the valley head
where a wet north-facing lintel of rock
has cornered and cupped enough of the wind
for dripping water to freeze. Icicles:

once, I unrooted some six-foot tusk
from the waterfall's crystalized overhang,
lowered it down and stood it on end, then stared
at an ice age locked in its glassy depths,
at far hills bottled in its weird lens.

These are brittle and timid and rare, and weep
in my gloved fist as I ferry them home.
I'd wanted to offer my daughter
a taste of the glacier, a sense of the world
being pinned in place by a diamond-like cold
at each pole, but I open my hand
and there's nothing to pass on, nothing to hold.

Nurse at a Bus Stop

The slow traffic takes a good long look.
Jilted bride of public transport,
alone in the shelter,
the fireproof bin and shatterproof glass
scrawled with the cave art of cocks and hearts.

It's late, Friday, the graveyard shift, you're ready
to dab blood from a split lip,
to hold the hand of cancer till the line goes flat.

Cardigan, sensible shoes, the kids
with a neighbor, fob watch pinned
like a medal to your breast.

Winter sharpens the day.
The centuries crawl past,
none of them going your way.

Emergency

The four-pump petrol garage
finally closed,
its defeated owner
inhaling his ghost
in a disused quarry
by coupling the lips of his car exhaust
to the roots of his lungs
via a garden hose.

On the bulldozed forecourt
they threw up a tram shed
for decommissioned emergency vehicles
where a skeleton workforce
services all manneration
of mothballed workhorses
for occasional call-outs
to sitcoms, period dramas, and film sets.

And the actual fire station
is up for rent,
that chapel-shaped building
where they stabled the one engine,
spit-buffing and wire-wooling
the chrome fenders,
T-Cutting the steel coachwork
to a flame red;

so what you see,
as the letting agent puts it,
is what you get:
boot cupboard, functional kitchenette,
brass hooks—two still holding
a brace of yolk-yellow plastic helmets—
northlight roof windows
and inspection pit.

The makeshift crew
were volunteer part-timers:
butchers, out-menders,
greasy perchers and hill farmers
who'd pitch up in bloody aprons,
boiler suits or pajamas
then venture forth,
fire-slaying on the tender,

and sometimes in dreams
my fire-fighting forefathers
appear, cosmonaut-like,
breathing from oxygen cylinders
through a sudden parting
of towering black cumulonimbus
on fully telescoped
turntable ladders.

The bank's gone as well,
and also the post office,
though in the store-cum-off-licence
you can sign a gyro
with a string-and-sellotape-tethered
half-chewed biro

or deface a scratchcard
or sell a bullmastiff.

The horizon ablaze—
is it moor-fire or sundown?
In the local taproom
prescription jellies and tin-foil wraps
change hands under cover
of *Loot* magazine
and Tetley beer mats.
What is it we do now?

Poundland

Came we then to the place abovementioned,
crossed its bristled threshold through robotic glass doors,
entered its furry heat, its flesh-toned fluorescent light.
Thus with wire-wrought baskets we voyaged,
and some with trolleys, back wheels flipping like trout tails,
cruised the narrow canyons twixt cascading shelves,
the prow of our journeying cleaving stale air.
Legion were the items that came tamely to hand:
five stainless-steel teaspoons, ten corn-relief plasters,
the Busy Bear pedal-bin liners fragranced with country lavender,
the Disney design calendar and diary set, three cans of Vimto,
cornucopia of potato-based snacks and balm for a sweet tooth,
toys and games, goods of Orient made, and of Cathay,
all under the clouded eye of CCTV,
beyond the hazard cone where serious chutney spillage had occurred.
Then emerged souls: the duty manager with a face like Doncaster,
mumbling, "For so much, what shall we give in return?"
The blood-stained employee of the month,
sobbing on a woolsack of fun-fur rugs,
many uniformed servers, spectral, drifting between aisles.
Then came Elpenor, our old friend Elpenor,
slumped and shrunken by the Seasonal Products display.
In strangled words I managed:
    "How art thou come to these shady channels, into hell's ravine?"
And he:
    "To loan sharks I owe the bone and marrow of my all."
Then Walt Whitman, enquiring politely of the delivery boy.
And from Special Occasions came forth Tiresias,
dead in life, alive in death, cider-scented and sockless,
Oxfam-clad, shaving cuts to both cheeks.

And my own mother reaching out, slipping a tin of stewing steak
to the skirt pocket of her wedding dress,
blessed with a magician's touch, practiced in need.

But never until the valley widened at the gated brink
did we open our lips to fish out those corn-colored coins,
those minted obols, hard-won tokens graced with our monarch's
    head,
kept hidden beneath the tongue's eel, blood-tasting,
both ornament and safeguard, of armor made.
And paid forthwith, then broke surface
and breathed extraordinary daylight into starved lungs,
steered for home through precincts and parks scalded by polar
    winds,
laden with whatnot, lightened of golden quids.

Maundy Thursday

Right royally we'd screwed up,
        splashed out
                on non-essential starches and yeasts,

spreed through a month's wage
        one Wednesday night
                till emptied pockets

hung loose and sad like donkeys' ears.
        So we stooped low
                at the fountain of dreams,

filched pounds and pence
        from tiled shallows,
                coins bleached to a minted gleam,

money tossed by the moneyless
        fishing for money,
                ground-bait scattered for love, hope,

reprieve from tumor and so forth.
        And such nickel and brass
                was treasure enough

in the night-bus driver's open palm:
        nursed, we were,
                in the double-decker's swaying cot,

incubated in amber light,
        rocked toward
                morning's lampwick

and narrow streets. Tipped out
        I stole home
                through a back door,

wet feet wearing casts of cold,
        proper skint, flayed hands
                mittened with chlorine's taint.

The Empire

True, it wasn't the Berlin Philharmonic but it paid the rent.
McGuire served cakes and drinks on a silver tray,
made his own doilies but had to be watched with the change.
A cross-Channel swimmer, Jenkins tickled the keys in his sleep.
And I kept time on the snare: the clockwork of waltzes, fox-trots,
sometimes an eight-hour shift without missing a beat.

At night, graceful couples floated and glided wall to wall,
and never a foot out of line or a wrong move.
But the afternoons were a snake pit of shame and sleaze:
fake shoes given a quick shine with a sleeve;
charmers, chancers, carpet-baggers and bits on the side;
Altrincham widows trussed with knicker elastic and pins.

The last straw was a wide boy in white socks
whose lady-friend squealed as his hands traveled south.
He pulled her onto his hips, then behind her back
looked me full in the face, ran his ring finger
under his nose, breathed deep and mouthed the word CUNT.

That was the year they lowered the great chandelier
into a wooden crate and a mirror-ball swung in its place.
The world turned and went its thousand crazy ways.

The Review

Like half-dressed hospital patients stepping outside
for a smoke we waited under the lamppost, coned
in its wigwam of light, still an hour before dawn.
When the van pulled up my Jack pressed a coin
into the driver's palm and he sliced the nylon band
with his work knife and handed my Jack *The Times*.
Junk mail and supplements spilled to his feet
as he leafed through. Obituaries, crosswords,
a female aid worker shot by a passerby.
Then his eyes fixed on his own name, and his face shone
in the glow of the words, in the glare of praise;

a pharaoh's mask found by the strike of a match.

Back in the house he threw back a shot
of some precious Scotch he'd been saving for this.
Then he slept, unknown for an hour or two more
but ready to wake with the world reaching out
for his touch. My Jack: the heart
I'd nourished and nursed, the wounds I'd tended,
the knuckles I'd bandaged and kissed.

Then I swept all that was mine into a knotted sheet
and left him to part the blackout curtains alone,
to open his arms and welcome the oncoming blaze,
his golden future written on morning's page.

A Bed

Unmade, mid-morning.
A dress where it fell, where you snaked from it.
The slab of the bedsheet, marbled with creases.

These pillows washed up
along the strand-line. Plunder. Salvage?
The end of the world beyond its edge.

The patch of grass where we took down the tent.
A gift—the gift-wrap disturbed,
the present taken.

The quilt rolled back,
the wave not broken, always breaking.
The book left open, the page you were reading.

A Chair

All on its lonesome. Itself solitary.
Hieroglyph of the detainee.
This dining chair, the four bare legs,

orphaned foal, turned to the wall.
An armchair slumps, exhausted, tired of the wait.
This high chair implores to be lifted, held.

Compare the sofa or corny settee,
the cushioned togetherness, the chummy repose.

Then pity the chair. The meal for one.
Throne of the snubbed. After the inquiry.
Hooded and bound, fully confessed.

The policeman takes off his helmet.
The consultant closes the door.
Yourself only. Sit down. A chair.

Tractors

It's not far to the abbey,
half a day's stroll
through the head of the valley,

a trodden path
between tethered horses
and harvested crops.

But fifty-odd tractors
come cutting across,
some vintage contraptions

with boneshaker tires
that have ploughed through two wars,
some futuristic new-fangled types

kitted out
for a nuclear winter
or life on Mars, driven

by fifty-odd farmers
in curly pink wigs
and pink frilly bras,

with pink balloons
and pink satin ribbons
tied to their front forks

and towing-bars,
all for a good cause.
Tractors, tractoring

nose to tail.
So we wait on the verge
for the age it takes

a nurse to deliver the X-ray plate.
Then a doctor points
with his streamline Parker or Paper Mate

and we stare and stare
at the musket ball
or distant star

in your left breast.
There's no stately home anymore
or even a drive,

just a stranded gatehouse
or former lodge;
in an upstairs window

a small girl flattens
her face to the glass,
waves at the fifty-odd tractors

then waves at us,
mouthing wildly
as we drift past.

Miniatures

A washing line strung between our house and theirs,
those neighborly neighbors, settlers
from a lost age and a childless planet.

     In this flashback scene
I'm the kid sprawled on their front-room carpet
     staging shows and plays
with the sugar-glazed Capodimonte pieces
in the opera house of their hearth and fireplace:

the reclining shepherd, the snooty princess,
the drunken soldier, the tramp on the bench,
     the pig in the trough
     and the rearing horse,
every figure worth a fortnight's wages.

*

Teaspoon. Tack. Spokeshave. Bit.
Thimble. Bradawl. Crochet hook.

*

For my twenty-first I hunted down
a first edition of George Mackay Brown's
     Fishermen with Ploughs
with the netted shoal and plough at rest
     on the brick-colored cover,
     and handed it over.

Then they handed it back, gift-wrapped
in waxy brown paper and gardening twine
with a fiver, like a bookmark, slipped inside.

*

The apple seller.
A wren in its nest.
The poised ballerina.
The scribe at his desk.

*

When I lift the lid of the model village
they're just as I left them, tinkering, grafting.

The king in his kingdom
of hen-scratched earth, a soft flurry
of Rhode Island Reds around his work boots,
or alone in the shed among oil-guns and ratchets,
hunched and wordless.

The queen in the gathered light of the porch
knotting coasters, doilies,
cushion covers and christening bonnets
with a worn tortoiseshell tatting shuttle
and fish-eye needles.
Or through veils of steam, glistening and ghostly,
rising from the cellar draped in laundry,
the yard a surrender
of boil-washed sheets and pillowcases.
I see white paper, clean pages.

Gravity

October on Earth
        and distinctly autumnal,
the goldfish bowl
        of the sixth-form common room,
an hour's lull
        in the space-time continuum

between double physics
        and English literature,
a radio oozing
        uninsistently
with American soft rock
        and easy listening,

a blurred ruckus
        of alpha males
working line-out drills
        and rolling mauls
with a Hallowe'en pumpkin,
        meeker souls

in tight constellations,
        some brown-nosing
through Isaac Newton
        or Robert Browning,
some Rubik's-cubing
        or grooming and braiding,

some lost in the coma
       of late revision.
As Fleetwood Mac's "Sara"
       looped the horizon
(the six-minute-plus
       album version)

the school trickster
       and first-choice scrum-half
plunged the volume slider
       from seven to nought
on the cusp of the line:
       "You're the poet in my heart."

And the airspace that followed
       was instantly baubled
with orbs and globes
       from the mouths of angels
and an outed choirboy's
       helium bubbles,

till the heavens ballooned
       with unworldly apples.

"Tiny"

Simon has taken his father, Peter,
       to the town's museum on No Through Road
to see for himself the world's smallest dog.
       Six inches at most from his mouse's nose
to the tip of his outstretched paintbrush tail,
       "Tiny" was born to pedigree pointers
of true proportion the same year Lassell
       discovered Triton—Neptune's largest moon—
and Britannia stole the Mountain of Light.
       He was raised as a regular working hound
but at three years old chased a rat down a hole,
       caught a fatal chill and was later embalmed.
Under a glass dome, skewbald and well groomed,
       he's tracking a scent through a diorama
of matchstick fence-posts and pipe-cleaner trees;
       a warped sky of roof beams and lightbulbs swims
in the bulged, unblinking eye of the case.
       Simon says, "Do you think he's real? I think
he's real—look at the fine nap of his coat."
       But Peter is elsewhere now, admiring
an Iron Age mattock, a chunk of quartz,
       and a nineteenth-century fishing skiff,
actual size. For only twenty pence
       the clockwork tin mine stutters into life.

Privet

Because I'd done wrong I was sent to hell,
down black steps to the airless tombs
of mothballed contraptions and broken tools.
Piled on a shelf every daffodil bulb
was an animal skull or shrunken head,
every drawer a seed tray of mildew and rust.
In its alcove shrine a bottle of meths
stood corked and purple like a pickled saint.
I inched ahead, pushed the door of the furthest crypt
where starlight broke in through shuttered vents
and there were the shears, balanced on two nails,
hanging cruciform on the whitewashed wall.

And because I'd done wrong I was sent
to the end of the garden to cut the hedge,
that dividing line between moor and lawn
gone haywire that summer, all stem and stalk
where there should have been contour and form.
The shears were a crude beast, lumpen, prewar,
rolling-pin handles on Viking swords,
an oiled rivet that rolled like a slow eye,
jaws that opened to the tips of its wings
then closed with an executioner's lisp.
I snipped and prodded at first, pecked at strands,
then cropped and hacked, watching spiders scuttle
for tunnels and bolt-holes of woven silk,
and found farther in an abandoned nest
like a begging bowl or a pauper's wreath,
till two hours on, the hedge stood scalped
and fleeced, raw-looking, stripped of its green,

my hands blistered, my feet in a litter
of broken arrows and arrowhead leaves.

He came from the house to inspect the work,
didn't speak, ran his eye over the leveled crown
and shorn flanks. Then for no reason except
for the sense that comes from doing a thing
for its own sake, he lifted me up in his arms
and laid me down on the top of the hedge,
just lowered me onto that bed of twigs,
and I floated there, cushioned and buoyed
by a million matchwood fingertips,
held by nothing but needling spokes and spikes,
released to the universe, buried in sky.

Prometheus

My job was to watch and listen and wait.
Written-off cars stacked six or seven high
formed a shadowy slum of ginnels and lanes
and the whole scrapyard had slowed to the clock
of fatigued metal ticking down into rust.
Crippled axles lay junked in a loose pile.
A butchered chassis swung from the crane's hook.
A telephone rang on an outside bell
and rang and rang and a threadbare guard dog
chained to a mangled Ford Cortina
pawed at an upturned plastic bowl and yawned.
The telephone rang. With its headlights popped
and its bonnet sprung one vehicle gawped
with the death-shriek of its fatal shunt.

A rough cinder track made bloody by rain.
Down which he jogged, my father, rushed me
out through the gate and along the street, then slowed,
then stopped at the corner and opened his hand.
A priceless spark plug sat in his palm,
loomed in the space between my face and his:
the machined gunmetal bullet-shaped tip,
the molded tooth-colored porcelain cap
with CHAMPION branded across it in red,
the threaded steel shaft, and below it a gap
where the two electrodes didn't quite touch,
like the finger of man and the finger of God.
Within that divide, in the daylight there,
the glint in his eye, the makings of fire.

Harmonium

The *Farrand Chapelette* was gathering dust
in the shadowy porch of Marsden Church
and was due to be bundled off to the tip
or was mine, for a song, if I wanted it.

Sunlight through stained glass which on bright days
might beatify saints or raise the dead
had aged the harmonium's softwood case
and yellowed the fingernails of its keys,
and one of its notes had lost its tongue
and holes were worn in both the treadles
where the organist's feet in grey woolen socks
and leather-soled shoes had pedaled and pedaled.

But its hummed harmonics still struck a chord:
it had stood facing the choristers' stalls
where father then son had opened their throats
and gilded finches—like high notes—had streamed out.

Through his own blue cloud of tobacco smog,
with smoker's fingers and dottled thumbs
he comes to help me cart it away.
We lay it flat then carry it out on its back,
and him being him he has to say
that the next box I'll shoulder through this nave
will bear the load of his own dead weight.
And me being me I mouth in reply
some shallow or sorry phrase or word
too starved of breath to make itself heard.

I Kicked a Mushroom

and then I felt bad.
And not just some cute toadstool or gnome's bed
but a fruiting body of brain-colored disks
as wide as a manhole cover or bin lid,
a raft of silky caps basted in light rain
stemming from one root as thick as a wrist,
anchored in deep earth, like a rope on a beach.
One jab with a spade would have done the job,
then a pitchfork to hoik it over the hedge,
but I stuck in the boot then walked away
with its white meat caught in my tongue and lace.
All night it lies on the lawn inside out,
its tripes and corals turned to the stars,
gills in the air, showing the gods what I am.

The Keirin

Don't follow the Derny my old man said.
But I fell for the bubbling two-stroke song
in its throat, its purring petrol-fed heart,
and got caught up in its breeze, carried away
by its heavenly fumes and the promise
of fame, and pedaled along in its wake.

Oh Derny, contraption extraordinaire,
part classic lady's step-through bike,
part old-school motorized pacing machine
with its sensible chain-guard and fixed gear
and fuel tank perched on the handlebars.
Hypnotized by the black blur of its back tire,
nursed in the velodrome's oval embrace,
eight or nine of us slipstreamed in single file,
a circling pageant of carbon fiber,
strobing spokes and chrome, a seamless ride
along polished strips of Siberian pine.

Oh Mr. Derny with the upright stance
of a circus poodle driving a toy train,
in your tight black leggings and trackie top
and safety helmet like a walnut shell
you are Max Wall slash human cannonball
slash station porter slash traffic warden
slash cartoon burglar slash table magician
slash Ealing Hitler all rolled into one,
all you need is the spinning bowtie
and Chaplin moustache and a fragrant rose
that spunks water in an admirer's eye.

Oh Mr. Derny, be ye a Cornishman?
Are we heading for Truro or Praa Sands?
Will we coast among ruined mines, freewheel
down the Camel Trail's disused railway line
or wiggle our way to Porthcurno Bay
where transatlantic telegraph cables
leave for the New World, reach out for a new life?

Nose to tail around that barreled camber we roled,
twenty thousand faces painted like flags
roaring us on, but just when the Earth's orbit
had picked out the tune of my own heartbeat
he glanced backwards, old Derny, with vacant eyes
and a funeral director's bloodless smile,
then peeled away from the track, then vaporized.

It was simply a race to the death after that.
Full pelt along the final straight I passed
a gangly lad with a mouth full of sand,
his featureless lifeless soul lying sprawled
in the open grave of the long-jump pit.
And a pole-vaulter speared like a speared fish.

Snipe

I was minding my own,
      kicking along
            through beech mast

and leaf litter
      down by the pond
            when it spat into flight,

a head-shot triggered
      from ground level, a burst
            of rifle-straight bill

and chevroned wings—one wingtip
      feathered my temple.
            But no trace

of its skulking, no tripod footprints
      or needled mud, no lair or *scrape*
            where it had crouched, cocked

in the scrubby margin.
      No spent cartridge.
            I looked it up

in an old field guide:
      to aim a put-down
            or snide comment.

Single round,
　　　lone marksman,
　　　　　could have had my eye out.

The Making of the English Landscape

It's too late now to start collecting football shirts,
bringing them back from trips abroad as souvenirs:
the sun-struck God-given green and gold of Brazil;
Germany's bold no-nonsense trademark monochrome;
the loud red of "emerging nation" South Korea;

then hanging them framed, arms folded across the chest
to show off the collars and cuffs and the piped sleeves
and the proud badges, shield-shaped, worn on the left breast,
embroidered with flags or mottos or mythical beasts.

So I'll turn instead to matters closer to home,
to these charters, maps, and aerial photographs
of double ditches and heaped walls and lynchet banks,
of sheep trails still visible below city parks,
of drove roads contradicting four-lane motorways,
of super-farms underwritten by patchwork fields,
of capped wells, earthworks, middens, and burial mounds,
the skeleton seen through the flesh, an embedded
watermarked view of when we were nothing and few.

And from outer space this latest satellite image
taken just moments ago shows England at dusk,
its rivers cascading beyond its coast, the land
like a shipwreck's carcass raised on a sea-crane's hook,
nothing but keel, beams, spars, down to its bare bones.

An Inquiry into the Nature and Causes
of the Wealth of Nations

Compiling this landmark anthology of poetry in English
about dogs and musical instruments is like swimming through tar.
To date I have only "On the Death of Mrs. McTuesday's Pug,
Killed by a Falling Piano," a somewhat obvious choice.
True, an Aeolian harp whispers alluringly
in the background of the anonymous sonnet
"The Huntsman's Hound,"
but beyond that: silence.

I should resist this degrading donkey work in favor of my own
    writing
wherein contentment surely lies.
But A. Smith stares smugly from the reverse of the twenty-pound
    note,
and when my bank manager guffaws
small particles of saliva stream like a meteor shower
through the infinity of dark space
between his world and mine.

The Ice Age

Tuesday the tenth, Wakefield Westgate Station,
seven in the morning,
the north end of the southbound platform,

the platform itself
a long promenade overlooking the prison.
Frost scrimshawed on waiting-room windows,

every lungful of air
transmuted to silver,
commuters standing about like skittles.

And one skinny kid in jeans and trainers
and a purple glow-stick
worn as a choker

crouched in a patch of useless sunlight,
arms in his T-shirt,
hugging his body heat, shivering, yawning.

Take off your coat and hold it toward him.
Offer it knowingly,
brother to brother.

But he shakes his head, wants nothing from a man
with a train to catch and a coat to spare,
from the hundred-year-old

with the minted smile and retro shoes
and the ironed collar.
He says no, and your blood freezes over.

The Subconscious

Arrives with his daughter, she's all braced teeth
and blunderbuss freckles, she bolts
from the passenger seat
of his Fiat Doblò and gallops
with two dogs into the garden. It's Sunday.
Now suddenly here in his hand

the awkward contraption:
steel forks either end of a steel collar,
galvanized spring and trigger,
toothed prongs that snap down—
he throws back his head—it's instant.
The girl and dogs play chase

near the birdbath. The lawn's a bomb site.
He strides between conical mounds
of fresh soil, probes the turf
with a wooden dabble,
intrudes into dark tunnels
with a silver trowel—see,

the walls are rounded and fossil-smooth
as if burrowed by serpents—
lowers four primed traps,
tamps down loose earth
then marks each site
with a metal rod flying a colored ribbon.

He knows my sister.
One dog's a pet, the grey one's a ratter.
A week on Monday
he's back on his own.
It's snowed, he scrapes it away
with his instep, raises

three traps choked with dirt, in the fourth
something hangs in the jack-knifed pincers,
a soft cosh or limp rubber tube
or a stuffed sock—that's how it looks
from the bedroom window.
He tosses it into a Hessian sack, the mini-flagpoles

slide into a quiver. The doorbell.
He takes off his gloves, offers a pink hand.
He does wasps, vermin, I wouldn't believe
the damage caused by a single roe deer.
When he's gone I pitchfork
frozen volcanoes into the tractor-trailer.

Beach Wedding

From the scalloped door of the seaside church
they often spill out onto the beach
for photographs: unearthly beings, the bride
an apparition of satins or silks
among stripy towels and inflatable sharks,
the groom in a morning suit, walking the sand
in bare feet wearing his shoes on his hands.

She'll hitch her dress as far as her garter,
he'll carry her ten yards into the water.
Heading out for Atlantis they pause here
on the point of departure; her long train
floats on the surface and drifts and darkens.

Some empty evenings a figure arrives
in a shooting jacket and combat trousers,
combing the shore with a metal detector,
sweeping for coins or keys, grubbing for rings.
The shovel hooked to the back of his belt
drags behind him like a devil's tail.
Herring gulls loot the bird-proof litterbins.

Before first light a spring tide visits and leaves,
panning for gold, re-setting the scene,
while under a thin sheet husband and wife
lie badly wounded after the first fight.

The Unthinkable

A huge purple door washed up in the bay overnight,
its paintwork blistered and peeled from weeks at sea.
The town storyteller wasted no time in getting to work:
the beguiling eldest girl of a proud bankrupt farmer
had slammed that door in the face of a freemason's son
who then bulldozed both farm and family
over the cliff, except for the girl, who lives now
by the light and heat of a driftwood fire on a beach.

There was some plan to use the door as a jetty
or landing stage, but it was all bullshit, the usual idle talk.
That's when he left and never returned. Him I won't name,
not known for his big ideas or carpentry skills,
a famous non-swimmer, but last seen sailing out,
riding the current and rounding the point in a small boat
with tell-tale flashes of almost certainly purple paint.

Deor

Weland the goldsmith   knew grief's weight.
That strong-minded man   was no stranger to misery,
his loyal soul mates   were sorrow and longing,
a hurt like winter   weathered his heart
once Niðhad had hamstrung   and hobbled his hopes,
fettering the feet   of the worthier fellow.
As that passed over   may this pass also.

Beadolid was bereft   at the death of her brothers
but distressed more deeply   by difficulties of her own.
Once the unthinkable   thought had occurred,
that a child grew inside her,   then her sanity dissolved
and imagined misfortunes   muddled her mind.
As that passed over   may this pass also.

We are told the tale   of troubled Mæðhilde,
Geat's much-loved   lovesick lady;
disturbing dreams   dispossessed her of sleep.
As that passed over   may this pass also.

For thirty long winters   the warlord Theodric
held the fort of the Mærings,   his fame known to many.
As that passed over   may this pass also.

Word reaches our ears   of Eormanric,
lupine-minded,   a merciless lord,
ruler of the Goths   in remote regions.
Many a man   sat manacled by sorrow,
awaiting the end   but wishing always
for that fearful tyrant   to fall in defeat.
As that passed over   may this pass also.

Pitiful he sits,   deprived of all pleasure,
his soul diminished,   his spirit dimmed,
believing ill luck   limitless.
Then a man's mind   might muse awhile
on the ways of our Lord   in this wide world,
how He favors many   with fame or fortune,
sends sweetness to some,   suffering to others.
And a little of myself   I should like to say now:
honoured *skald*   in the House of Hoedening,
I was dear to my master   and my name was Deor.
Through several seasons   I was proud to serve him,
my loyal protector.   But the title and lease
I once held as my own   he has handed on
to Horrender, poet   of a higher order.
As that passed over   may this pass also.

To-Do List

- Sharpen all pencils.
- Check off-side rear tire pressure.
- Defrag hard drive.
- Consider life and times of Donald Campbell, CBE.
- Shampoo billiard-room carpet.
- Learn one new word per day.
- Make circumnavigation of Coniston Water by foot, visit Coniston Cemetery to pay respects.
- Achieve Grade 5 Piano by Easter.
- Go to fancy dress party as Donald Campbell complete with crash helmet and life jacket.
- Draft pro forma apology letter during meditation session.
- Check world ranking.
- Skim duckweed from ornamental pond.
- Make fewer "apple to apple" comparisons.
- Consider father's achievements only as barriers to be broken.
- Dredge Coniston Water for sections of wreckage/macabre souvenirs.
- Lobby service provider to unbundle local loop network.
- Remove all invasive species from British countryside.
- Build 1/25 scale model of Bluebird K7 from toothpicks and spent matches.
- Compare own personality with traits of those less successful but more popular.
- Eat (optional).
- Breathe (optional).
- Petition for high-speed fiber-optic broadband to this postcode.
- Order by express delivery DVD copy of *Across the Lake* starring Anthony Hopkins as "speed king Donald Campbell."
- Gain a pecuniary advantage.

- Initiate painstaking reconstruction of Donald Campbell's final seconds using archive film footage and forensic material not previously released into public domain.
- Polyfilla all surface cracking to Bonneville Salt Flats, Utah.
- Levitate.
- Develop up to four thousand five hundred pounds/force of thrust.
- Carry on regardless despite suspected skull fracture.
- Attempt return run before allowing backwash ripples to completely subside.
- Open her up.
- Subscribe to convenient one-a-day formulation of omega oil capsules for balanced and healthy diet.
- Reserve full throttle for performance over "measured mile."
- Relocate to dynamic urban hub.
- Eat standing up to avoid time-consuming table manners and other non-essential mealtime rituals.
- Remain mindful of engine cut-out caused by fuel starvation.
- Exceed upper limits.
- Make extensive observations during timeless moments of somersaulting prior to impact.
- Disintegrate.

October

All day trimming branches and leaves, the home owner
sweeping the summer into a green heap;
all evening minding the flames,
inhaling the incense of smoldering laurel and pine.

Or careering home from school down Dog Shit Lane
between graves and allotments,
the old churchwarden propped on a rake
in a standing sleep, bent over a fire
of cut flowers and sympathy cards and wreaths.

Solitary

Pacience is a poynt, þaȝ hit displese ofte.

I think of Robert Maudsley in his glass case,
on his cardboard chair, next to his concrete bed.
Like a blind man hearing a mouse, his blank face

half-turned towards me then stared into space.
A cardboard plate offered a slice of concrete bread.
I think of Robert Maudsley in his glass case:

"Given half a chance he'll spoon out your brains
through your ears and eat them raw," the warden said
of the bland mousy man with the blank face.

All day platform announcements at Wakefield chase
along prison landings, down stone steps,
into the ears of Robert Maudsley in his glass case;

all night freight trains and sleeper trains
crawl through a man's mind as he sits and reflects.
Like a blind mouse hearing a man, my face

half-turns towards Wakefield when the radio says
he's still there, in the same cell, locked in his head.
I think of Robert Maudsley in his glass case,
his blank face looking back at his blank face.

Avalon

To the Metropolitan Police Force, London:
the asylum gates are locked and chained but undone
by wandering thoughts and the close study of maps.
So from San Francisco, patron city of tramps,
I scribble this note, having overshot Gloucester
by several million strides, having walked on water.

City of sad foghorns and clapboard ziggurats,
of snakes-and-ladders streets and cadged cigarettes,
city of pelicans, fish bones, and flaking paint,
of underfoot cable-car wires strained to breaking point.

I eat little—a beard of grass, a pinch of oats—
let the salt-tide scour and purge me inside and out,
but my mind still phosphoresces with lightning strikes
and I straddle each earthquake, one foot either side
of the fault line, rocking the world's seesaw.
At dusk, the Golden Gate is heaven's seashore:
I watch boats heading home with the day's catch
or ferrying souls to glittering Alcatraz,
or I face west and let the Pacific slip
in blazing glory over the planet's lip,
sense the waterfall at the end of the journey.

I am, ever your countryman, Ivor Gurney.

The Claim

Working the mountain, working the mine,
operation mind-fuck: I am one man.

All that I own I've sunk into these seams,
everything staked, upholding the old ways,
chasing the grain and the sleek green dream
of flawless tombstones at rest in the slate.

Some days the ears play tricks on the mind.
Or is the mind playing tricks on the ears:
birdsong, sirens singing my name?
Then some shitty old Herdwick ambles along
(a sheep—this far in, this far down!) and kneels
on a high ledge over the hollowed dome,
a natural cavern I've christened The Great Hall.

The bedrock sweats. The mountain holds its breath:
not once in its hundred million years
has it filled its lungs or emptied its chest.

I've stopped wearing a watch, just toil and truck
till thinness of blood or thinness of thought
call time on the shift, then wander back up.

And stumbled out once into snow, to a vision
of clear night skies and profound whiteness asleep
on the ground, into which I walked and was risen.

The Holy Land

Christ was born under Tinsley Viaduct—
why not?—
the Leopold being overbooked.

They dipped him in the silver waters
of the Don
until his little hands were forks.

Magi brought gifts from as far away
as Carnaby
and Goole: hair straighteners,

a replica Louis Vuitton man-bag, a two-piece
snooker cue.
Herod's henchmen sought him out,

hoodies from Bethlehem, PA, but hidden
in a battered
velvet-lined guitar case our Saviour slept.

In his teenage years he underachieved
but showed
promise in team sports, especially lacrosse.

Pointing to the seven hills he proclaimed:
"There shall I
picnic, there shall I BMX, preach,

sip Special Brew at dusk, find a cure
for cancer
of the lung, walk the dog, and there

on a goalpost shall they nail-gun my palms
and feet."
He asked us, "Who is your Lord? Who's

the big fella around here? Into whose arms
shall you turn?"
We answered, "Thee. Thou. Thine."

Camera Obscura

This eight-year-old sitting in Bramhall's field,
shoes scuffed from kicking a stone,
too young for a key but old enough now
to walk the short mile back from school.

He's spied his mother down in the village
crossing the street, purse in her fist.
In her other hand her shopping bag nurses
four ugly potatoes caked in mud,

a boiling of peas, rags of meat or a tail of fish
in greaseproof paper, the price totted up
in penciled columns of shillings and pence.
How warm must she be in that winter coat?

On Old Mount Road the nearer she gets
the smaller she shrinks, till he reaches out
to carry her home on the flat of his hand
or his fingertip, and she doesn't exist.

Kitchen Window

You wanted more view, more day. So out
came the heavy sashes and beveled frames,
the dulled soft-focus cataracts of old glass,
and the counterweights—dumbbells of crude iron
hanging on frayed ropes—all thrown in the skip.

Wrapped in a canvas sheet the brand-new pane
rode on the side-rack of the joiner's van.
Undressed and carried, cloudscapes tilted
in its mirror and the planet swayed, though
set in place it seemed a solid nothingness—
a panel of air or frozen light
that magnified its own transparency.

Simian, almost, in nature and name,
I could swing up onto the outside ledge
and hunch in the angle of wall and lintel,
my ankle hooking a plastic bucket half-filled
with a lukewarm broth of bloated sponges and cloths
and a slimy liver of chamois leather
for swabbing the glaze.

                From inside the house
the hummingbird of your hand and finger
pointed or tapped at streaks and smears, or your face
came close to the brink to mouth instructions
then fell away behind net curtains.
Then fell away farther, sinking to deeper
darker reaches and would not surface.

Old Boy

Nothing surprises me now, nothing at all:
a severed arm in the bottle bank; electricity owned by the
   French . . .
Our friends the bees have packed their yellow-and-black
   carpetbags
and are leaving the planet for a better home.

My neighbour the DJ keeps twenty thousand popular songs
on some little thingamajig he wears on a gold chain
round his neck. "All the thoughts you've ever thunk could fit
into this," he tells me, and he has no reason to fib.

Why must you leave your glasses case in my favorite chair?
Is it too much to request that the forks lie separate from the knives?
If I have asked once I have asked a hundred thousand times
regarding green apples, pork crackling, and the like.

A dancing bear from a flooded valley in the foothills I am relocated
to the city of This Morning and cruelly set free. In times of drought
the chimney stack and the church steeple puncture the reservoir.
A monkey with a jigsaw I contemplate the day.

Poor Old Soul

"You'll enjoy it," I say, when the carer arrives
and wants to wheel him to the park. I watch him
puzzling with the leather buttons
on his favorite coat, fingers like sticks of chalk.

Coming home from a week abroad I find him
hunched and skeletal under a pile of clothes,
a Saxon king unearthed in a ditch.
"I ran out of biscuits," he says,

"and the telly's on—I couldn't make it stop."
When I throw back the curtains, morning
bursts like a water balloon before he can rig up
his tatty umbrella of epidermis and bone.

Portrait of a Maharajah

Whole towns were painted ocean blue
to welcome him, but he stayed home.

The tooth of a great white shark
implanted in his lower jaw actually took root
and grew, ditto the fingernail of a dead saint.

Despite rumblings to the south
his only acknowledged enemy was the grey squirrel.

In a staring competition with the carved head of a demigod
the stone statue was the first to blink.

If lamb rogan josh in a king-size Yorkshire pudding
was what he wanted, lamb rogan josh
in a king-size Yorkshire pudding was what he got.

Where other people kept toilet tissue,
fresh-killed still-warm albino conies
made a sorrowful pile.

He introduced the Bengal tiger
to the lower Pennines but with limited success.

On the one occasion he wept, his bottled tears
were shipped under armed escort to Jerusalem and Rome.

According to legend, during lovemaking
he assumed the form of an English Longhorn bull.

To his one son he gifted the clouds above
and grazing rights along Spurn Point.

In the allotments by the railway sidings he dozes,
flies unbuttoned, powdered egg on his shirt,
a wheelbarrow for a bed.

The Candlelighter

From Dove Cottage I sloped out through the side gate
and climbed the corpse road past the Coffin Stone,
then curved through a mixed copse to a scree path
scored by rainwater into the hill's back.
I was hauled upwards by a borrowed dog
on a makeshift leash, a yellow Labrador
gunning for every birdcall and blown leaf.
Over a hand-stacked wall, in the next fold,
under the driftwood bones of a late elm
a red deer had dropped down from the fell
with morning beaconed in its flaming horns.
With dawn-light cradled in its branching crown.
I stood in some blind spot of its dark eye
and deer and dog were still and unaware
and stayed that way, divided by the wall:
wild stag and hunting hound in separate worlds,
before the deer pushed on through tinder thickets,
igniting the next field. And the dog yawned.
Then I hacked up the ghyll to higher ground
counting the hikers striding along the ridge,
thinking of taking a drink from the tarn,
thinking of adding a new stone to the cairn.

The Cinderella of Ferndale

It was all about shoes. In that small town
there was hardly a foot she hadn't dressed
or clamped and sized in the Brannock Device,
and barely a toe that hadn't blenched
at the force of her thumb as she prodded and pressed.

Not known for her lightness of touch,
riding home one night at the back of the bus
she'd bungled a big tin of Dulux gloss
and a lurid delta of scarlet sludge
had fanned as far as the driver's heels
to be walked by passengers onto the street.

Fifty years later those footprints still stand:
on pavements and curbs, over zebra crossings
and under the bridge, round the boating lake,
across the surgery's waiting-room floor,
through the chapel gates; footprints in fading red—
the same shade as her own front door.
Through which no Prince of Wales had ever stepped.

The Send-Off

A maiden aunt on your mother's side,
out of the old west, last of a lost tribe.

The town on the tilt: funicular streets,
wheelie bins padlocked to gutter pipes.

Mid-terrace, back room, the lino can't hide
the molehills and ruts of an earthen floor,

windows made of rain, the parlor a shrine,
the bathroom a lean-to afterthought,

the kitchen a coop with a Perspex roof,
stairs like steps cut into a hill,

the landing a scaffold, the bedroom door
a raft of floorboards braced with a hinge

and latched with the hasp from a garden gate.
We sleep in the deathbed, wake in a dirge

at the Chapel of Rest . . . *in pastures green;*
He leadeth me the quiet waters by.

The cars arrive and the cortege rolls
down a boulevard of Lottery signs,

through an esplanade of charity shops.
Some local muscleman walking his dog

drags his hat from his head as we crawl past.
Then a slow sweep through the cemetery gates,

past the burnt-out boarded-up sexton's house
to a huddled throng of waitresses' blouses

and golf umbrellas and prison shoes
and borrowed black ties and wedding suits.

So we pick out a path between slabs and tombs,
tottering, stint-like, stalking the mud,

the vicar calling us through to the front
to stand on the brink of the family plot.

Where the ground opens and swallows us up.

Redwoods

Ten or eleven grow
at the turn in the track
where the track doubles back
to tackle the slope.

Odd beings for these woods.
And still young, though they already stoop
over cypress and spruce
with the shame of the tall.

Dozens of times
we've given them names:
veterans in bloodied coats;
rogue astronomers; magi sworn

to a stillborn lord.
But see them this year
for what they are:
trees, nothing more,

thoughtlessly mute
and relentlessly dumb
whether we stand here talking, pointing,
or move on.

Glencoe

No one to warn me
    it was a dead end.
        Snow like a thrown sheet

over a lost friend.
    This folded promissory note,
        no use

to the tea-cozy grouse
    with its feathered bootees;
        no use to the royal stag.

I bed down in a stone pen
    and curl up unborn.
        Is it girls singing? An avalanche?

A blue fox
    steals a lick of salt
        from my hand.

Morning, a shepherd.
    The kiss of life
        from the lips of a flask.

But the night has set down
    its strict condition:
        no question, I'll come back.

Gymnasium

Loneliness regarding the treadmill,
pounding feet on a seamless rubber road,
eventless action, no perceptible shift
in relation to the given positions of planets and stars.
The inherent loneliness of the game of squash,
the observation cells of the cross-sectioned courts,
sterile laboratory light,
the ball itself formed of a bled heart
found in a hospital bin.
Loneliness as in nine muted TVs
showing golf in the desert. *The Desert Classic.*
The lifeguard in his ten-foot chair,
a beard-growing boredom set in,
a life sentence of scanning the deep
for flailing infants and turds.
Loneliness as in the taken-as-read,
single-handed-around-the-world loneliness
of the rowing machine. The loneliness
of dumb weights consisting only of weight.
The silent companionless scream of the castaway's mind
in the bodybuilder's head.
Loneliness swabbing the tiled changing-room floors,
the undisputable solitude of the mop.
The unreconstructed loneliness of shower blocks
and spent soap, the poverty of private parts
long after their best.
The girl at reception, post-Soviet, pale,
clocking off after a shift.
The loneliness of the minimum wage,
of a car park, a car,

the shops on the high street open this late,
Christmas for one, every item a pound, the loneliness
of the inside lane, the metronome
of intermittent windscreen wipers in light rain,
the drive for its own sake, the motorway service station
as a destination in its own right.

Violins

Christmas delivers us into the city of rain,
late-night shopping, the season in meltdown,
a last-minute gift. At the slow end of Deansgate
a Santa in trainers and jeans falls out of a tiled pub,
street light drips from Victorian brickwork,
a parking meter guzzles its supper of coins.

So we're shown upstairs then upstairs again,
a room at the back then the room behind that, call it
booth, cubby hole, studio, store, carpeted walls
to absorb the cries, another wall glazed
with aquarium glass—from across a hallway
a monocled clerk looks up from a ledger and blinks.

And here are the violins, the chess-piece bishops,
grouse and pheasant hung by their feet,
sea horses hooked by their scrolled heads, specimen beetles
pinned on a board—all thorax and craned neck—
four-eyed insects wearing their guts on the outside.
You lift one down from a wooden peg,

trigger its nerves with a faint brush of your sleeve,
coax agony out of the four taut strings,
touching its points of pain. A handwritten label
glimpsed in its hollow breast: the luthier's name, a whiff
of glue pots in workshops in Prague or Milan, a world
of lacquer and lathes, the turning of hand-cranked drills.

Call it cloakroom or pantry, here a cello carcass
leans on a chair, and here's a viola, abandoned, unlaced,

and you in that prison-blue dress now taking
another carapace down from the rack, your arm
sawing for notes, your hand at its throat
making it whimper then sing, but reaching again

for spruce, maple, rosewood, tortoiseshell, flame,
a darker model nursed in the crook of your arm
and cupped to your chin but this time too sharp,
and the next uncertain in tone, the wrong feel, back it goes,
the sound of a bolt sliding home, an alarm being set,
the manager checking his watch, the clerk in his coat—

you have to choose NOW, as your mother chose,
lifted you up to her cheek saying this one, my own violin,
and wrapped and bundled you out of that room of cribs.

Burrow Mump

I'm quite at home
with a book and a map,
and so taken in by the Blowing Stone
that I'm almost putting

my mouth to the hole;
whoever plays it—
if the note carries to White Horse Hill—
inherits the throne.

Which by turns leads me to Burrow Mump
and the half-built crown
of St. Michael's Church
with its circular view

of the wetland and drains
and flooded rhines
and droving lanes
of the Somerset Levels.

And I'm quite alone on that tor or toft,
in my stone coracle,
in St. Michael's palm,
when, trailing an arm,

I airlift my Susan
by hook or by crook
from the chimney pot of a sunken farm,
and we sail on.

On we sail,
backed all the way
by a gentle southerly
to beyond Othery.

At the Reading,
the Poet Introduces His Poem

It's good to be back in the city of _____.
City of hot-air balloons and bicycle shops.
City of iron bridges and boardwalks spanning the dry docks.

I lived here once. It was a secret life.
I made no phone calls, didn't answer the door,
paid always with cash, never by card or check.

In the mornings she dressed in the dark,
put her foot on the chest of drawers
as she pulled on her tights or laced her boots,

left coffee and bread in the room,
returned at dusk with hot ingots of takeaway food,
her pale hands wearing winter's white lace gloves.

Much has changed here. Entire roads no longer exist.
But the word *Mauritania* glows as it did
from a gable end, its letters on fire,

and wooden boats tie up as they please
at the feet of investment banks, thin ropes
threaded through metal hoops set into the street.

So I'll read for you now my _____ poem.
Where I once lived. Where the bedroom curtains
were drawn during the day and flung wide at night.

The Poet Hosts His Annual Office Christmas Party

I play Solitaire on the computer
and sweep the floor with myself.
To enhance the mood
I've strung fairy lights across the bookcase
and pinned a sprig of mistletoe over the door.

It's fancy dress and I've come as Björn Borg circa 1978—
the trademark headband
keeping my straggly blond fringe out of my eyes.
I pull down my tight white shorts,
sit on the flatbed scanner and photocopy my bits.

Swigged from the cap of the bottle
a small tot of single malt
eases the mind,
yet these flashing reindeer antlers
feel like a sparrowhawk perched on my scalp.

The art of pulling my own cracker
is something I've mastered over the years;
I win a plastic magnifying glass
and a funny joke about skeletons.
Trivia fact: Rudolph et al. must have been female

since the bulls of the species shed their horns
in early winter.
I have the beginnings of an idea
for a short unrhymed piece
about the melting of the polar ice caps,

but there's no way I'm putting pen to paper
right now, in my free time.
I climb on the desk and let rip with the guitar solo
to end all guitar solos, teased
from the strings of my traditional wooden racket.

The Kilogram

It still looks good enough to me, a squat lump
of platinum-iridium, triple-housed in a bell-jar dome
within a bell-jar dome within a bell-jar dome.
But its days as a weight belong in the past
having sweated a sand-grain of mass at least
in the hundred-plus years since it was first cast.

In the same room, other absolute constants
are laid out, even more neglected and sad.
The Volt, lying blank and flat, all but discharged.
The decayed Inch, a ghost of its former self.
And the Second, no longer coiled in its case
but sprung and buckled, sprawled all over the place.
God, as filmed on celluloid, bleached out by sun.
Love, the bloodstained tissues and the cherry stone.

Thank You for Waiting

At this moment in time we'd like to invite
First Class passengers only to board the aircraft.

Thank you for waiting. We now extend our invitation
to Exclusive, Superior, Privilege and Excelsior members,
followed by Triple, Double and Single Platinum members,
followed by Gold and Silver Card members,
followed by Pearl and Coral Club members.
Military personnel in uniform may also board at this time.

Thank you for waiting. We now invite
Bronze Alliance members and passengers enrolled
in our Rare Earth Metals Points and Reward Scheme
to come forward, and thank you for waiting.

Thank you for waiting. Accredited Beautiful People
may now board, plus any gentleman carrying a copy
of this month's *Cigar Aficionado* magazine, plus subscribers
to our Red Diamond, Black Opal, or Blue Garnet promotion.
We also welcome Sapphire, Ruby, and Emerald members
at this time, followed by Amethyst, Onyx, Obsidian, Jet,
Topaz, and Quartz members. Priority Lane customers,
Fast Track customers, Chosen Elite customers,
Preferred Access customers, and First Among Equals customers
may also now board.

On production of a valid receipt travelers of elegance and style
wearing designer and/or hand-tailored clothing
to a minimum value of ten thousand U.S. dollars may now board;
passengers in possession of items of jewelry

(including wristwatches) with a retail purchase price
greater than the average annual salary
of a mid-career high school teacher are also welcome to board.
Also welcome at this time are passengers talking loudly
into cellphone headsets about recently completed share deals,
property acquisitions, and aggressive takeovers,
plus hedge fund managers with proven track records
in the undermining of small-to-medium-sized ambitions.
Passengers in classes Loam, Chalk, Marl, and Clay
may also board. Customers who have purchased
our *Dignity* or *Morning Orchid* packages
may now collect their sanitized shell suits prior to boarding.

Thank you for waiting.
Mediocre passengers are now invited to board,
followed by passengers lacking business acumen
or genuine leadership potential, followed by people
of little or no consequence, followed by people
operating at a net fiscal loss *as* people.
Those holding tickets for zones Rust, Mulch, Cardboard,
Puddle, and Sand might now want to begin gathering
their tissues and crumbs prior to embarkation.

Passengers either partially or wholly dependent on welfare
or kindness: please have your travel coupons validated
at the Quarantine Desk.

Sweat, Dust, Shoddy, Scurf, Feces, Chaff, Remnant,
Ash, Pus, Sludge, Clinker, Splinter, and Soot:
all you people are now free to board.

The Unaccompanied

Wandering slowly back after dark one night
above a river, toward a suspension bridge,
a sound concerns him that might be a tune
or might not: noise drifting in, trailing off.

Then concerns him again, now clearly a song
pulsing out from the opposite bank, being sung
by chorusing men, all pewter-haired or bald,
in the function suite of a shabby hotel.
Above their heads a conductor's hand
draws and casts the notes with a white wand.

Songs about mills and mines and a great war,
about mermaid brides and solid gold hills,
songs from broken hymnbooks and cheesy films.

Then his father's voice rising out of that choir,
and his father's father's voice, and voices
of fathers before, concerning him only,
arcing through charged air and spanning the gorge.
He steps over the cliff edge and walks across.

Homework

It's evening again, late.
I go out into the lane
and doodle a beard and mustache
on the face of the moon
with a red pen.

Over the next hill
an old teacher of mine
takes off her glasses
and wipes the lenses with a soft cloth.
She can't believe
what she's just seen.

Simon Armitage was born in West Yorkshire and is Professor of Poetry at the University of Sheffield. A recipient of numerous prizes and awards, he has published eleven collections of poetry, including *Seeing Stars, Paper Aeroplane: Selected Poems 1989–2014,* and his acclaimed translation of *Sir Gawain and the Green Knight. The Shout: Selected Poems* was nominated for the National Book Critics Circle Award, and his translation of the medieval poem *Pearl* received the 2017 PEN Award for Poetry in Translation. He writes extensively for radio and television, has published three best-selling nonfiction titles, and his theater works include *The Last Days of Troy,* performed at Shakespeare's Globe in London. He has taught at the University of Iowa's Writers' Workshop and in 2015 was appointed Professor of Poetry at Oxford University.

.

A NOTE ON THE TYPE

The text of this book was set in Sabon, a typeface designed by Jan Tschichold (1902–1974), the well-known German typographer. Based loosely on the original designs by Claude Garamond (ca. 1480–1561), Sabon is unique in that it was explicitly designed for hot-metal composition on both the Monotype and Linotype machines as well as for filmsetting. Designed in 1966 in Frankfurt, Sabon was named for the famous Lyons punch cutter Jacques Sabon, who is thought to have brought some of Garamond's matrices to Frankfurt.

Composed by North Market Street Graphics,
Lancaster, Pennsylvania

Printed and bound by Thomson-Shore,
Dexter, Michigan

Designed by Soonyoung Kwon

3290